W9-BTR-577

When My Grandmother
Was a Child

MIDDLEPORT PUBLIC LIBRARY
MIDDLEPORT, OHIO 45760

MIDDLEPORT PUBLIC LIBRARY
MIDDLEPORT, OHIO 45760
DATE DUE

MAY 2 7 1996		
JUL 0 5 1996		
AUG 0 3 1996		
SEP 0 5 1996		
SEP 2 1 1996		
OCT 1 5 1996		
NOV 1 5 1996		
NOV 0 4 1999		

973.8/Rut

Rutledge, Leigh W.
When my grandmother was a ch
$12.95 LibPur 65998 MT 973.8

MEIGS COUNTY PUBLIC LIBRARY

T 65998

OTHER BOOKS BY LEIGH W. RUTLEDGE

Diary of a Cat

Dear Tabby

A Cat's Little Instruction Book

Cat Love Letters

It Seemed Like a Good Idea at the Time

The Lefthander's Guide to Life

Excuses, Excuses

The author's grandmother and
great-grandmother at the turn of the century.

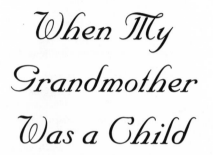

When My Grandmother Was a Child

LEIGH W. RUTLEDGE

MIDDLEPORT PUBLIC LIBRARY
MIDDLEPORT, OHIO 45760

A DUTTON BOOK

DUTTON
Published by the Penguin Group
Penguin Books USA Inc., 375 Hudson Street, New York, New York 10014, U.S.A.
Penguin Books Ltd, 27 Wrights Lane, London W8 5TZ, England
Penguin Books Australia Ltd, Ringwood, Victoria, Australia
Penguin Books Canada Ltd, 10 Alcorn Avenue,
Toronto, Ontario, Canada M4V 3B2
Penguin Books (N.Z.) Ltd, 182–190 Wairau Road, Auckland 10, New Zealand

Penguin Books Ltd, Registered Offices: Harmondsworth, Middlesex, England

First published by Dutton, an imprint of Dutton Signet,
a division of Penguin Books USA Inc.
Distributed in Canada by McClelland & Stewart Inc.

First Printing, April, 1996
2   4   6   8   10   9   7   5   3   1

Copyright © Leigh W. Rutledge, 1996
All rights reserved

Photo acknowledgments. Culver Pictures: pages 4, 7, 49; The Bettmann Archive: pages
17, 22, 25, 40, 45, 65, 72, 77, 81, 88, 91; Archive Photos: page 47.

 REGISTERED TRADEMARK — MARCA REGISTRADA

LIBRARY OF CONGRESS CATALOGING-IN-PUBLICATION DATA:
Rutledge, Leigh W.
When my grandmother was a child / Leigh W. Rutledge.
p.   cm.
ISBN 0-525-94105-3
1. United States—Social life and customs—1865–1918—Miscellanea.   I. Title.
E168.R9615   1996
973.8—dc20   95-25497
CIP

Printed in the United States of America
Set in Goudy, Nuptial Script and Bernhardt Modern
Designed by Eve L. Kirch

Without limiting the rights under copyright reserved above, no part of this publication
may be reproduced, stored in or introduced into a retrieval system, or transmitted, in any
form, or by any means (electronic, mechanical, photocopying, recording, or otherwise),
without the prior written permission of both the copyright owner and the above publisher
of this book.

This book is printed on acid-free paper. ∞

To my grandmother
Viola Marie
1892–1993

I 65998

Introduction

The past is a foreign country;
they do things differently there.
—L. P. Hartley

On June 25, 1900, as the Gilded Age was fading into memory and the country looked forward to the seemingly inevitable prosperity of a new century, my grandmother celebrated her eighth birthday at her parents' home in Cicero, Illinois.

She died, some 93 years later, at the age of 101, in a hospital in Carmel, California.

Sitting by her bedside during her final illness, I was occasionally stunned by thoughts of the astonishing breadth of her life, which very nearly spanned the entire twentieth century. It was startling for me to realize, for example, that when she was a child Queen Victoria, Mark Twain, Oscar Wilde, Rasputin, and Wyatt Earp were all still alive. Airplanes, antibiotics, and nuclear power were unheard of. The Panama

Canal had not been built, Mount Rushmore hadn't been carved, there was no United Nations, no one had climbed Mount Everest or Mount McKinley or even gone over Niagara Falls in a barrel, and Oklahoma, Arizona, and New Mexico hadn't been admitted to the Union yet. People were still, as a matter of habit, civil and gracious to one another; unlike today, they generally trusted the good intentions of neighbors and strangers. In short, the world was a compellingly different place.

My grandmother was an extraordinary woman, even beyond the way in which all grandmothers are extraordinary women in the eyes of their grandsons. Her generosity, her value system, the entire way she looked at the world, influenced me (and countless other people she knew) profoundly. Staying by her side at the end of her life, I began to wonder what there was in her background, in her upbringing, in the world in which she was raised, that would account for who she was and how she thought. The question was inevitably raised in my mind: Had the world been a better, more agreeable place at the beginning of this century than it appeared to be as we neared the end of it?

What finally persuaded me to look more energetically at that question was a photograph.

I have on the wall of my study a large photograph, taken in the late 1890s, of my grandmother when she was six or seven years old. She is dressed in a simple, rather nondescript smock. (It almost looks like a dressing gown.) Her hair is cut short, somewhat boyishly. In the picture, she is being held adoringly around the legs by her mother, my great-grandmother, and her cheek rests with obvious affection against her mother's forehead.

Every time I've looked at that photograph I've wished I could peer into it, as if it were a store window, and survey everything inside. I've wanted to see what was going on around my grandmother and great-grandmother as they stood there posing for the camera that day. Where had the picture been taken? Presumably in a studio, or perhaps at home. If one walked outside—just walked a few feet from where the two of them were standing—what would one have seen? What would one have heard? How did the world smell and act and amuse itself?

Aside from my personal curiosity about these things, the world of my grandmother's childhood seemed like an ideal reference point to render a series of likenings and contrasts to the present, all the more compelling as we near the end of what has arguably been the most progressive and rambunctious century in the history of civilization. This then is a book of verbal "snapshots," reality postcards, of what an eight-year-old must have seen and experienced at the turn of the last century, during the long-ago summer of 1900.

*In the summer of 1900,
when my grandmother
was a child . . .*

The average life expectancy
in the United States
was forty-seven.

The fastest way to travel
between New York City
and San Francisco
was by train.
The trip took four days.
By boat, the same trip took
more than two months.
There was no Panama Canal.

Only 14 *percent of the homes
in the United States
had a bathtub.*

Telephone operators were
commonly referred to
as "hello girls."

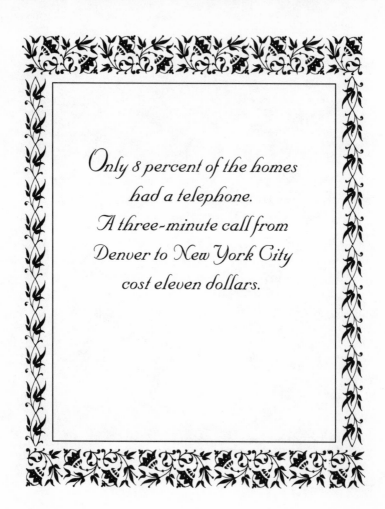

Only 8 percent of the homes
had a telephone.
A three-minute call from
Denver to New York City
cost eleven dollars.

There were only 8,000 cars
in the United States
and only 144 miles
of paved roads.
The maximum speed limit in
most cities was ten mph.

Despite the recent advent of automobiles, runaway horses were still a major problem on many city streets, with rampant animals occasionally galloping through store windows, trampling innocent bystanders, and tossing passengers into gutters, ditches, and mud holes. When a careless man in Denver, Colorado, left six small girls unattended in a horse-drawn wagon outside a downtown general store, the horse panicked and galloped off in a frenzy. The wagon careened, driverless, through several blocks of the downtown area, bouncing the girls, one at a time, into the road. All six were injured, and the horse was finally stopped only when a crowd of quick-thinking men formed a human barrier across the street.

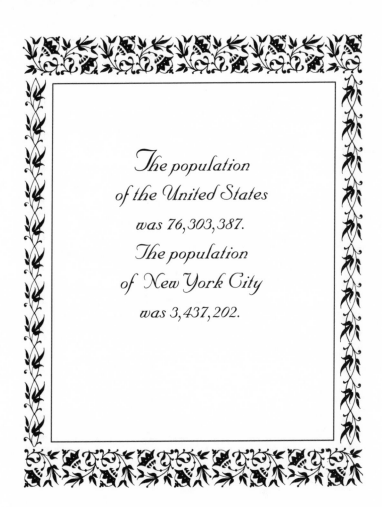

The population
of the United States
was 76,303,387.
The population
of New York City
was 3,437,202.

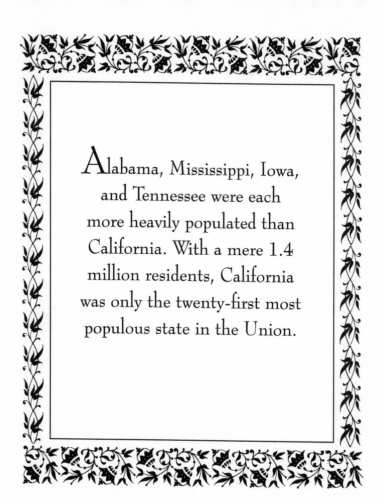

Alabama, Mississippi, Iowa, and Tennessee were each more heavily populated than California. With a mere 1.4 million residents, California was only the twenty-first most populous state in the Union.

There were more than one
million veterans of the
Civil War still alive.

The recently introduced Kodak Brownie camera sold for one dollar and a roll of film for fifteen cents. Amateur photographers were derogatorily referred to as "Kodakers." The frenzy surrounding amateur photography was quickly becoming so intense that newspapers and magazines began decrying the "promiscuous" overuse of cameras. "It sometimes seems," declared one indignant editorial, "as if the possession of a Kodak . . . means the departure of all good breeding from its owner." Especially obnoxious, the editorial noted, was the growing army of young women photographers who would jump out in front of famous people and take quick candid photos of them.

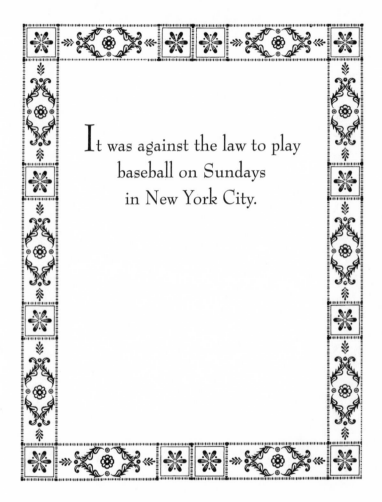

It was against the law to play
baseball on Sundays
in New York City.

Coca-Cola contained
cocaine instead of caffeine.

All Classes, Ages
and Sexes

DRINK

Coca-Cola

The Satisfactory Beverage

It satisfies the thirst and pleases the palate. Relieves the fatigue that comes from over-work, over-shopping or over-play. Puts vim and go into tired brains and bodies.

Cooling-Refreshing-Delicious, Thirst-Quenching

Guaranteed under the Pure Food and Drugs Act, June 30, 1906. Serial No. 3324

5c. Everywhere

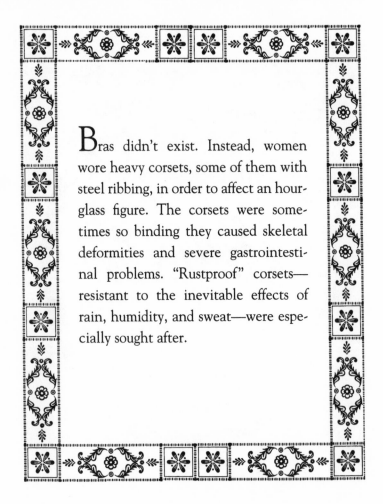

Bras didn't exist. Instead, women wore heavy corsets, some of them with steel ribbing, in order to affect an hourglass figure. The corsets were sometimes so binding they caused skeletal deformities and severe gastrointestinal problems. "Rustproof" corsets—resistant to the inevitable effects of rain, humidity, and sweat—were especially sought after.

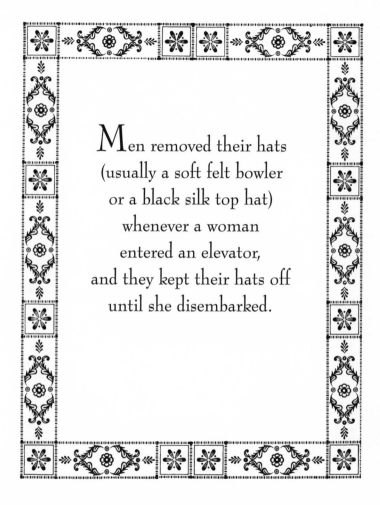

Men removed their hats
(usually a soft felt bowler
or a black silk top hat)
whenever a woman
entered an elevator,
and they kept their hats off
until she disembarked.

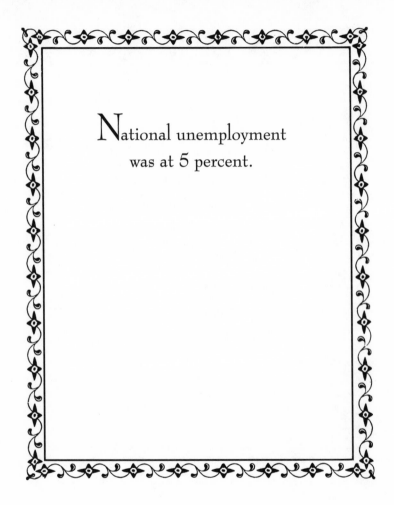

National unemployment
was at 5 percent.

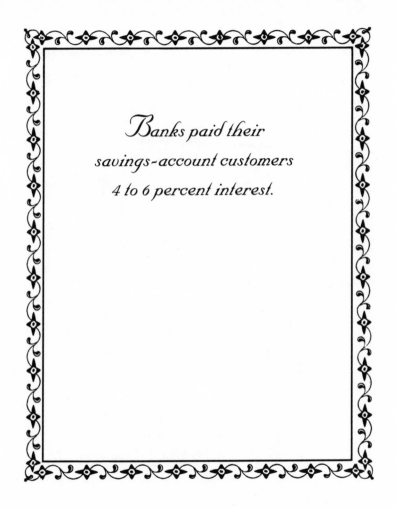

*Banks paid their
savings-account customers
4 to 6 percent interest.*

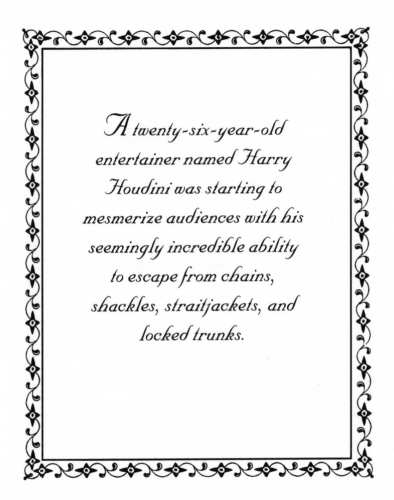

A twenty-six-year-old entertainer named Harry Houdini was starting to mesmerize audiences with his seemingly incredible ability to escape from chains, shackles, straitjackets, and locked trunks.

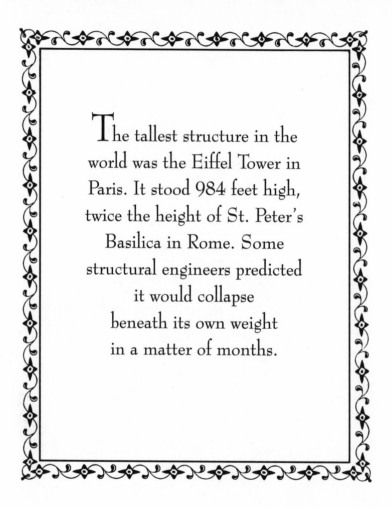

The tallest structure in the
world was the Eiffel Tower in
Paris. It stood 984 feet high,
twice the height of St. Peter's
Basilica in Rome. Some
structural engineers predicted
it would collapse
beneath its own weight
in a matter of months.

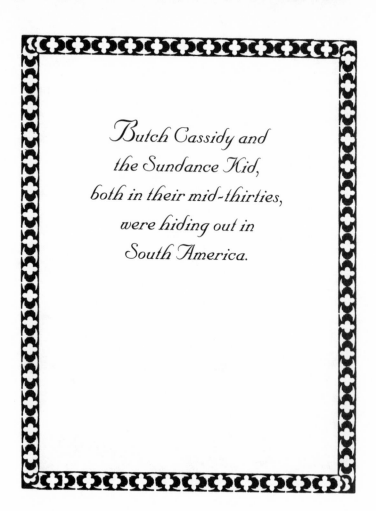

*Butch Cassidy and
the Sundance Kid,
both in their mid-thirties,
were hiding out in
South America.*

The most popular fad in the United States was the recently introduced cakewalk dance, in which participants walked to music around a large floor marked with chalk squares. Whoever was on a specially marked square when the music stopped won a cake or other baked delicacy.

Sigmund Freud was forty-four, working in Vienna, and had just published *The Interpretation of Dreams*. Physicist Max Planck was forty-two, working in Berlin, and had just elucidated the theoretical foundations of quantum mechanics. Both would turn the new century on its ear, one by saying the mind was full of ambiguities and difficult to comprehend, the other by saying the universe was full of ambiguities and *impossible* to comprehend.

The United States had no
official national anthem.
"The Star Spangled Banner,"
though written in the early
1800s, had not been
officially adopted as
the nation's anthem yet.

One in twelve U.S. marriages ended in divorce. In South Carolina, divorce was illegal. In some states, ministers refused to marry anyone who had been previously divorced. "I do not propose to prostitute my conscience for a few pieces of silver by making such unions," declared one irate minister in Cheyenne, Wyoming.

*A chocolate sundae
cost ten cents;
a root beer float
was five cents.*

"Flower missions"—similar to soup kitchens, but for the distribution of flowers to the poor and the homeless—were common in most major U.S. cities. The first one had been started in 1869 by Helen Tinkham, who, returning to Boston after a long weekend in the country, was moved to pity by all the homeless people who came up to her and admired the bundles of flowers she'd brought back with her. Flowers, it suddenly occurred to her, might brighten up their bleak lives considerably. By 1900, in Chicago alone, 170,000 bouquets were being distributed annually to tenement dwellers and other indigents throughout the city. Flowers were donated from private gardens, and then made into bouquets and distributed by church volunteers. In some cities, the endeavor expanded to include the distribution of ice cream as well.

*Only four states—
Wyoming, Idaho, Utah, and
Colorado—had given
women the vote.*

The average wage in
the United States was
twenty-two cents an hour.
The average U.S. worker
made between 200 dollars
and 400 dollars a year.

A competent accountant
could expect to earn
2,000 dollars a year,
a dentist 2,500 dollars a year,
a veterinarian between
1,500 dollars and
4,000 dollars a year,
and a mechanical engineer
about 5,000 dollars a year.

More than 95 percent of all births in the United States took place at home.

Ninety percent of all U.S. physicians had no college education. Instead, they attended medical schools, many of which were condemned in the press and by the government as "substandard."

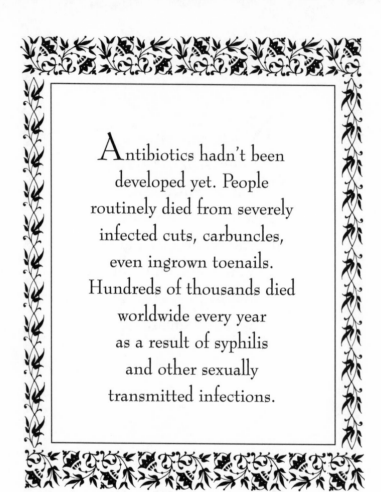

Antibiotics hadn't been
developed yet. People
routinely died from severely
infected cuts, carbuncles,
even ingrown toenails.
Hundreds of thousands died
worldwide every year
as a result of syphilis
and other sexually
transmitted infections.

*China painting and
lace making were two of
the most popular pastimes in
the country.*

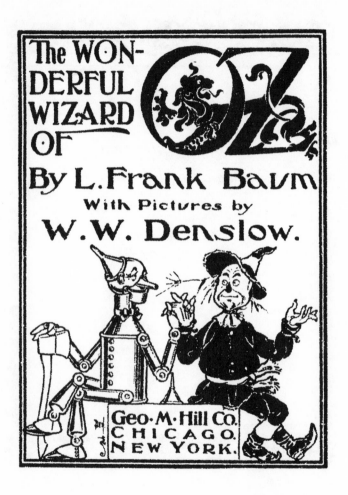

The WONDERFUL WIZARD OF Oz

By L. Frank Baum

With Pictures by

W.W. Denslow.

Geo. M. Hill Co.
CHICAGO.
NEW YORK.

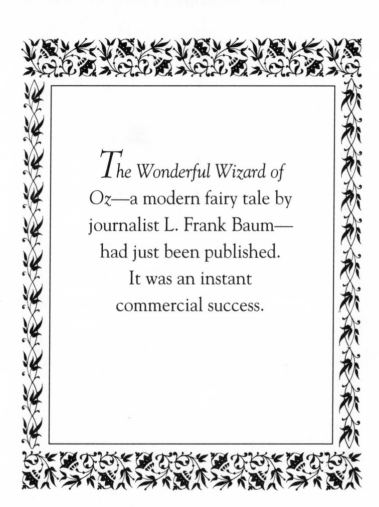

The Wonderful Wizard of Oz—a modern fairy tale by journalist L. Frank Baum— had just been published. It was an instant commercial success.

Almost every city park
in America had a carousel.

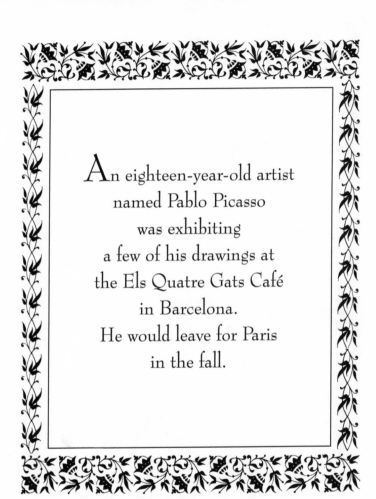

An eighteen-year-old artist
named Pablo Picasso
was exhibiting
a few of his drawings at
the Els Quatre Gats Café
in Barcelona.
He would leave for Paris
in the fall.

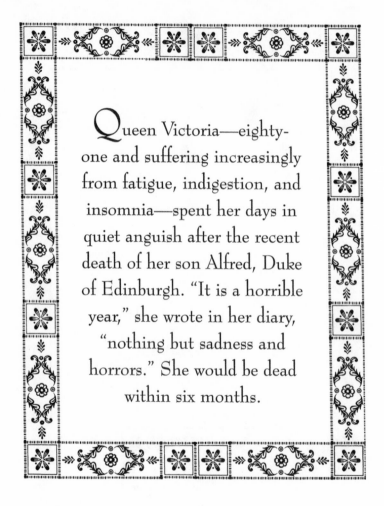

Queen Victoria—eighty-one and suffering increasingly from fatigue, indigestion, and insomnia—spent her days in quiet anguish after the recent death of her son Alfred, Duke of Edinburgh. "It is a horrible year," she wrote in her diary, "nothing but sadness and horrors." She would be dead within six months.

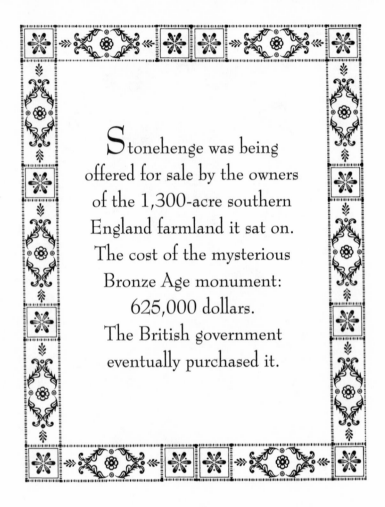

Stonehenge was being
offered for sale by the owners
of the 1,300-acre southern
England farmland it sat on.
The cost of the mysterious
Bronze Age monument:
625,000 dollars.
The British government
eventually purchased it.

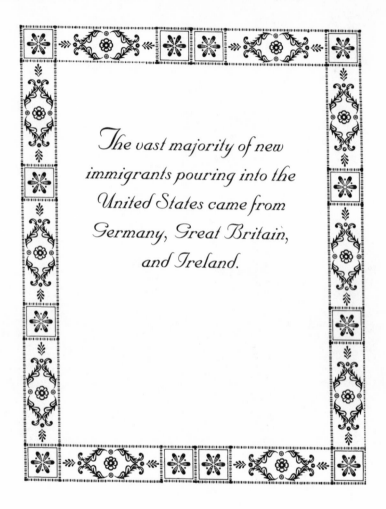

The vast majority of new immigrants pouring into the United States came from Germany, Great Britain, and Ireland.

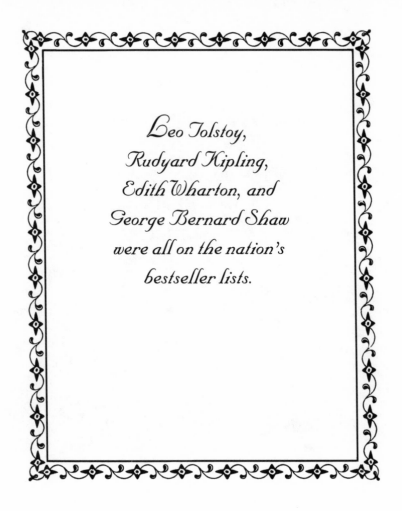

Leo Tolstoy,
Rudyard Kipling,
Edith Wharton, and
George Bernard Shaw
were all on the nation's
bestseller lists.

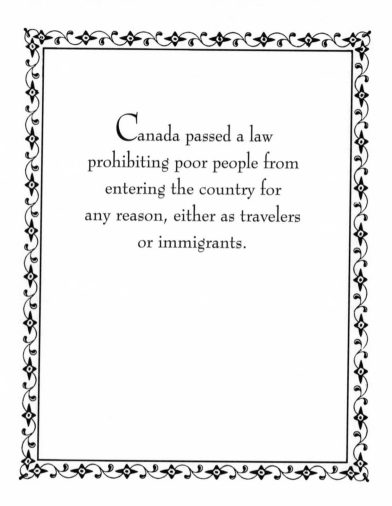

Canada passed a law
prohibiting poor people from
entering the country for
any reason, either as travelers
or immigrants.

Sugar cost four cents
a pound.
Eggs were fourteen cents
a dozen.
Coffee cost fifteen cents
a pound.

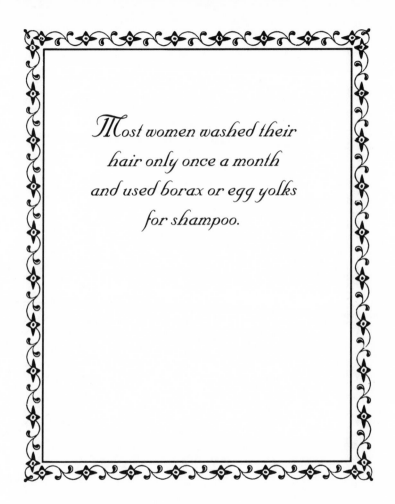

Most women washed their
hair only once a month
and used borax or egg yolks
for shampoo.

Baking soda was often
applied to the armpits
as a deodorant.

Journalists in New Mexico uncovered the strange case of an elderly blind woman, Mrs. R. Corbin, who was looking for gold in the desert outside Santa Fe. Mrs. Corbin, the widow of a miner who had devoted his life to searching for a reputed Spanish treasure in the area, would tie herself with long ropes to her tent every day and then crawl across the desert searching with her hands for telltale signs of the buried cache. Her story made national headlines.

"*A Bird in a Gilded
Cage*"— a song about a
beautiful but unloved woman
who feels trapped in her
lavish surroundings—
was the number-one song in
the country.

A popular sign in
U.S. theaters read:
"Don't spit on the floor.
Remember the
Johnstown flood."

Troop Train Crossing the Veldt—a brief black-and-white film clip showing a train in motion—was being exhibited at Keith's Biograph Theatre in New York City. Films were still in their infancy (and were generally regarded as a frivolous novelty by the public), and rarely ran more than five or ten minutes long.

The annual U.S. federal budget was 550 million dollars. There was no federal budget deficit. Most of the federal government's operating revenues came from liquor taxes. There was no federal income tax and no Internal Revenue Service.

The five leading causes
of death in the
United States were:

1. Pneumonia and influenza
2. Tuberculosis
3. Diarrhea
4. Heart disease
5. Stroke

Women could be arrested
for smoking in public
in New York City.

The vast majority of cheerleaders at football games were men and were usually injured or substitute players who tried to whip up enthusiasm (most often with a megaphone) among the spectators. The idea of female cheerleaders (whose sole purpose would be to entertain and energize fans) hadn't occurred to sports promoters yet.

*Cats were so much in vogue
they were used to advertise
everything from tar soap
to hosiery.
Kitty litter hadn't been
developed yet.
Most household cats were
encouraged to spend as much
time as possible outside.*

A fifty-four-year-old Kansas housewife, Carrie Nation, began her national crusade against bars and drunkenness when she armed herself with bricks and marched into a local saloon, announcing, "Men, I have come to save you from a drunkard's fate!" She began hurling the bricks at every bottle in sight and within minutes had demolished the saloon's entire inventory.

The American flag had
only forty-five stars.
Arizona, Oklahoma,
New Mexico, Hawaii, and
Alaska hadn't been
admitted to the Union yet.

Renowned Western lawman
Wyatt Earp was fifty-two,
his gun-toting days were
behind him, and he was
struggling to make
ends meet running a
saloon in Nome, Alaska.

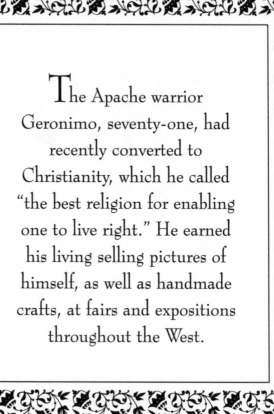

The Apache warrior Geronimo, seventy-one, had recently converted to Christianity, which he called "the best religion for enabling one to live right." He earned his living selling pictures of himself, as well as handmade crafts, at fairs and expositions throughout the West.

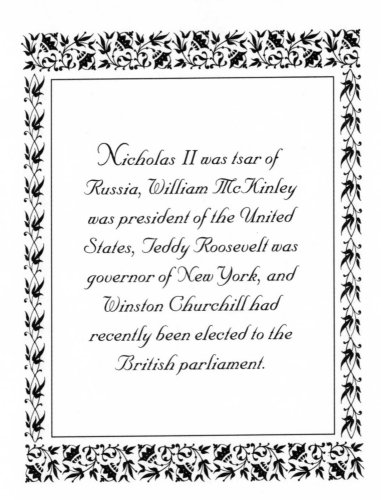

Nicholas II was tsar of Russia, William McKinley was president of the United States, Teddy Roosevelt was governor of New York, and Winston Churchill had recently been elected to the British parliament.

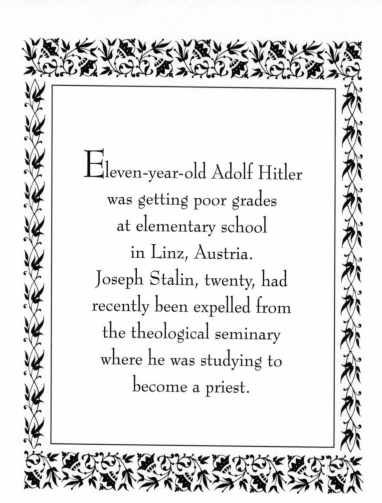

Eleven-year-old Adolf Hitler
was getting poor grades
at elementary school
in Linz, Austria.
Joseph Stalin, twenty, had
recently been expelled from
the theological seminary
where he was studying to
become a priest.

Utilities millionaire Cornelius Billings held a lavish party for the New York Riding Club at the sumptuous Louis Sherry Restaurant in Manhattan. Members entered the restaurant on horseback and ate dinner off silver trays while still astride their animals. The horses were served fresh oats, and a steady stream of young men dressed as jockeys cleaned up the ongoing mess behind the horses.

There were fewer than
1,000 buffalo left
in the United States,
down from an estimated
40 million of them
100 years earlier.

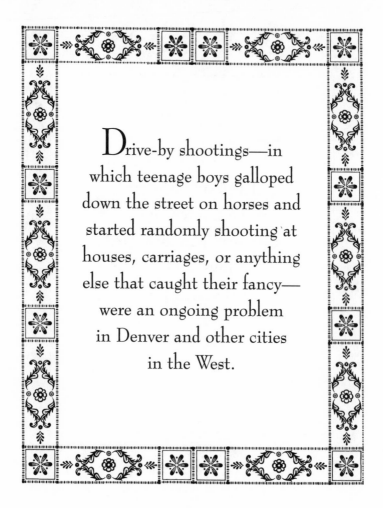

Drive-by shootings—in which teenage boys galloped down the street on horses and started randomly shooting at houses, carriages, or anything else that caught their fancy— were an ongoing problem in Denver and other cities in the West.

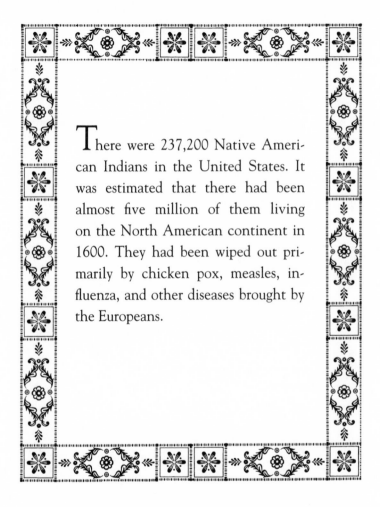

There were 237,200 Native American Indians in the United States. It was estimated that there had been almost five million of them living on the North American continent in 1600. They had been wiped out primarily by chicken pox, measles, influenza, and other diseases brought by the Europeans.

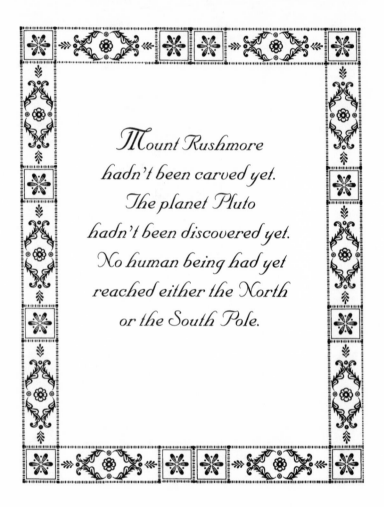

*Mount Rushmore
hadn't been carved yet.
The planet Pluto
hadn't been discovered yet.
No human being had yet
reached either the North
or the South Pole.*

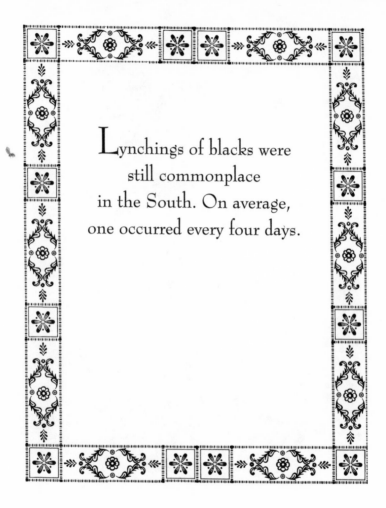

Lynchings of blacks were
still commonplace
in the South. On average,
one occurred every four days.

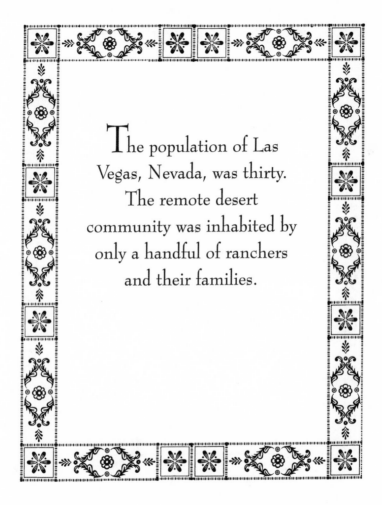

The population of Las Vegas, Nevada, was thirty. The remote desert community was inhabited by only a handful of ranchers and their families.

*The Statue of Liberty was
only fifteen years old.*

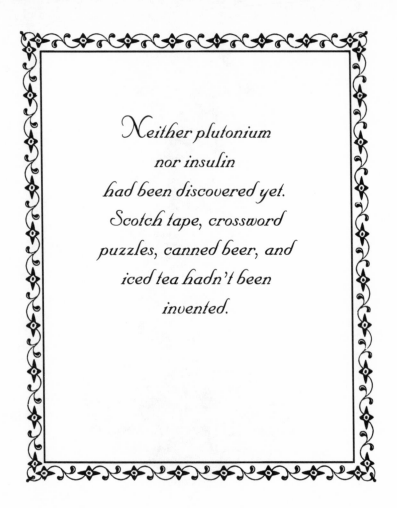

*Neither plutonium
nor insulin
had been discovered yet.
Scotch tape, crossword
puzzles, canned beer, and
iced tea hadn't been
invented.*

The most destructive
weapon in the world
was the black-powder shell
from a fourteen-inch mortar.
It was capable of destroying a
single large house;
though even with its
unprecedented explosive
force, it usually left one or
two outside walls standing.

The average American family had three children. The largest known family in the country was that of Mr. and Mrs. Samuel Swartwood of Wilkes-Barre, Pennsylvania. They had twenty-seven children. "And I tell you there was not one too many," Mrs. Swartwood told a reporter. "We welcomed them all and were glad they came."

There was no Mother's Day
or Father's Day.
The two holidays wouldn't be
invented for more than
a decade.

The growing craze for bicycling, especially among young women, drew sharp criticism from some social observers who found it unladylike. "After bicycling for any length of time," one writer complained, "many ladies find their wrists ache so much as to render pianoforte playing well-nigh impossible!"

Orville and Wilbur Wright,
twenty-nine and thirty-three
respectively, were building
their first glider
in North Carolina.
The first sustained powered
airplane flight would come
three years later.

Vaudeville "strong men"—performing unlikely feats of strength in front of astonished audiences—were popular in theaters across the United States. William Pagel drew gasps carrying horses up and down twelve-foot ladders. Paul von Boeckmann amazed audiences by doing chin-ups while hanging from a bar by only one finger. Eugene Sandow, perhaps the most popular of the strong men, enjoyed lifting several members of the audience at a time over his head with only one hand.

Sarah Bernhardt, at fifty-four still the most beloved actress in the world, was playing the title role of an eighteen-year-old youth, the Duke of Reichstadt, in Edmond Rostand's new play *L'Aiglon*, in Paris. "The Great Sarah . . . fails to metamorphose a woman over fifty into a youth of eighteen," one critic noted. "For Sarah is growing old—in looks, in voice, and in manner. And it would be rendering her a signal service to convince her of the fact." Later in the year, she would make her motion picture debut in a short film titled *Hamlet's Duel*. She would play Hamlet.

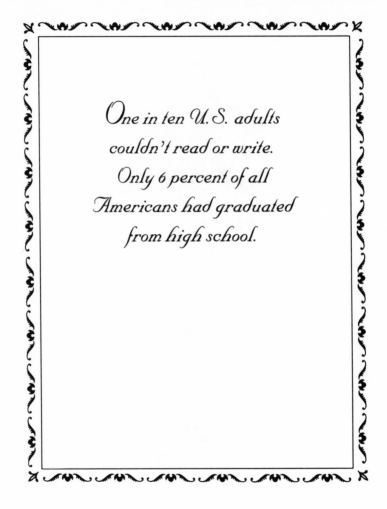

One in ten U.S. adults
couldn't read or write.
Only 6 percent of all
Americans had graduated
from high school.

*A first-class postage stamp
was two cents; a postcard
stamp was one cent.*

Newspapers still regularly printed the comings and goings of local residents: "Mr. Franklin Swann is quite ill at his home, at 1290 Greenbriar Street." "Mrs. J. P. Sharpless has left today for a long visit with her sister who lives in San Francisco." "Mr. Samson Sweeney and family have just returned from a pleasant three-day outing at Green Mountain Falls."

*Seventy million telegrams
were sent annually over more
than one million miles
of telegraph lines.*

Miss Annie Segall, a New York City woman traveling cross-country, was reported in national newspapers as having "gone insane" while waiting for a train in Kansas City, Missouri. The young woman—who reportedly paced around the depot for hours and who wrote out dozens of unsent telegrams (no one ever knew to whom they were addressed)—was an employee of the New York Public Library and was said to be fluent in French, Italian, Spanish, and German. The newspapers attributed her dementia to "overstudy."

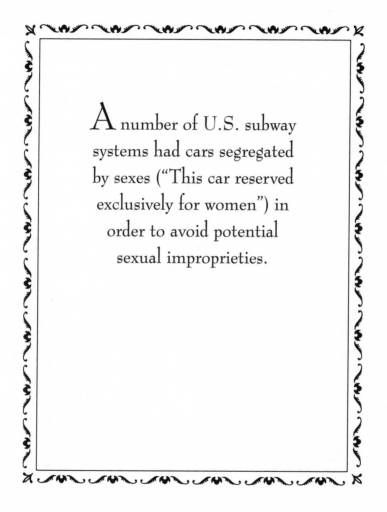

A number of U.S. subway systems had cars segregated by sexes ("This car reserved exclusively for women") in order to avoid potential sexual improprieties.

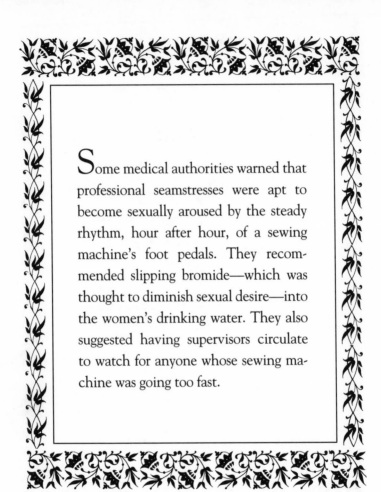

Some medical authorities warned that professional seamstresses were apt to become sexually aroused by the steady rhythm, hour after hour, of a sewing machine's foot pedals. They recommended slipping bromide—which was thought to diminish sexual desire—into the women's drinking water. They also suggested having supervisors circulate to watch for anyone whose sewing machine was going too fast.

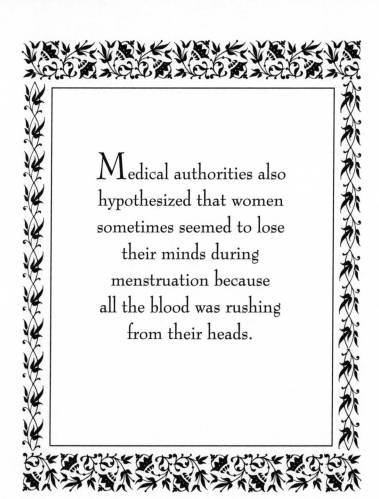

Medical authorities also hypothesized that women sometimes seemed to lose their minds during menstruation because all the blood was rushing from their heads.

People in mixed company said, "I'll be jiggered," instead of "I'll be damned."

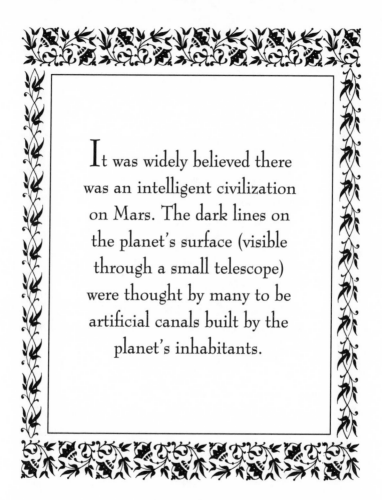

It was widely believed there was an intelligent civilization on Mars. The dark lines on the planet's surface (visible through a small telescope) were thought by many to be artificial canals built by the planet's inhabitants.

MIDDLEPORT PUBLIC LIBRARY
MIDDLEPORT, OHIO 45760

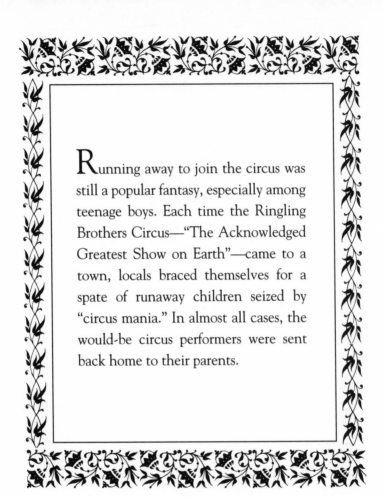

Running away to join the circus was still a popular fantasy, especially among teenage boys. Each time the Ringling Brothers Circus—"The Acknowledged Greatest Show on Earth"—came to a town, locals braced themselves for a spate of runaway children seized by "circus mania." In almost all cases, the would-be circus performers were sent back home to their parents.

*Phonographs played
cylinders instead of records
and had to be wound up
instead of plugged in.*

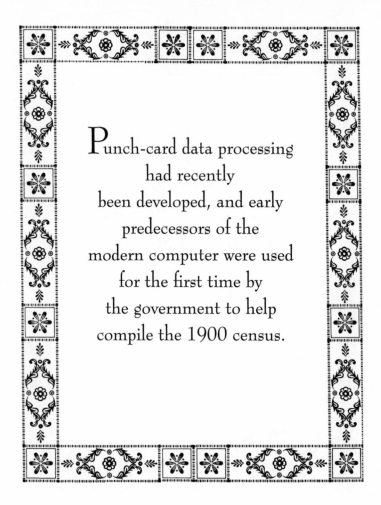

Punch-card data processing had recently been developed, and early predecessors of the modern computer were used for the first time by the government to help compile the 1900 census.

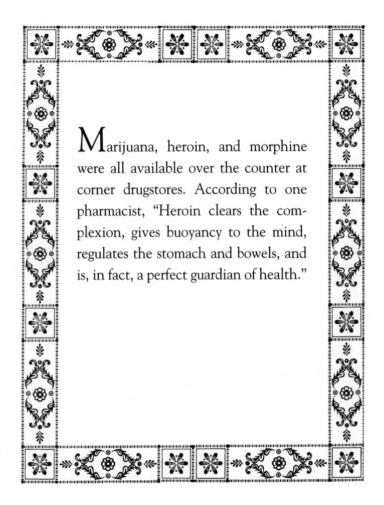

Marijuana, heroin, and morphine were all available over the counter at corner drugstores. According to one pharmacist, "Heroin clears the complexion, gives buoyancy to the mind, regulates the stomach and bowels, and is, in fact, a perfect guardian of health."

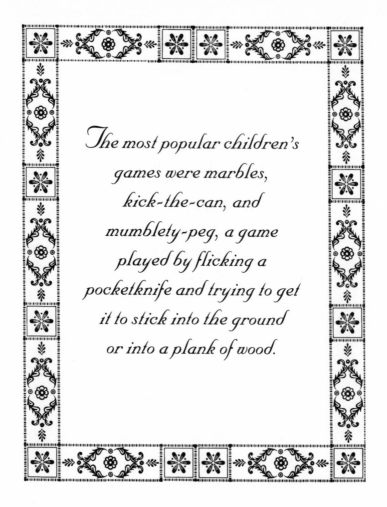

The most popular children's
games were marbles,
kick-the-can, and
mumblety-peg, a game
played by flicking a
pocketknife and trying to get
it to stick into the ground
or into a plank of wood.

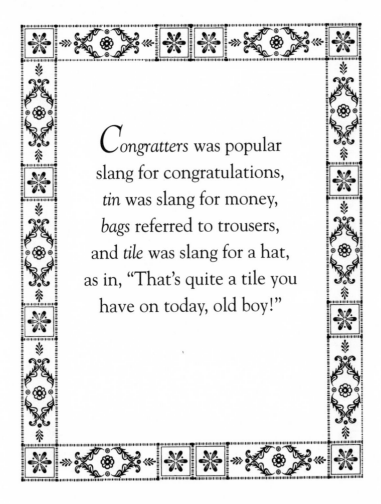

Congratters was popular slang for congratulations, *tin* was slang for money, *bags* referred to trousers, and *tile* was slang for a hat, as in, "That's quite a tile you have on today, old boy!"

Black businessman Charles Graves—president of the Gold Leaf Consolidated Mining Company of Montana—reported his net worth at over one million dollars, thus becoming the first black millionaire in U.S. history.

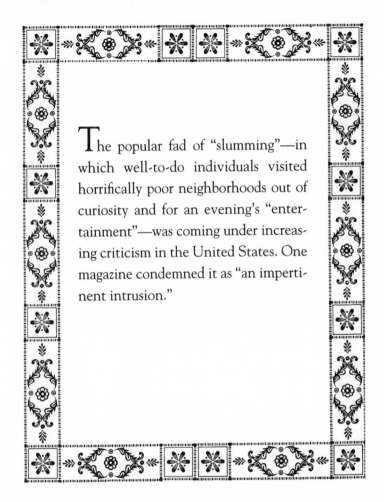

The popular fad of "slumming"—in which well-to-do individuals visited horrifically poor neighborhoods out of curiosity and for an evening's "entertainment"—was coming under increasing criticism in the United States. One magazine condemned it as "an impertinent intrusion."

*There were three
federally funded
leper colonies,
one in Louisiana
and two in Hawaii.*

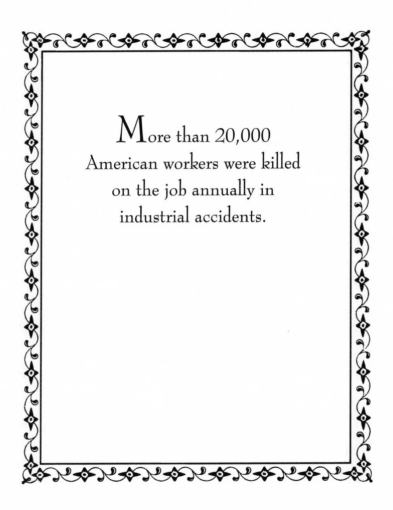

More than 20,000
American workers were killed
on the job annually in
industrial accidents.

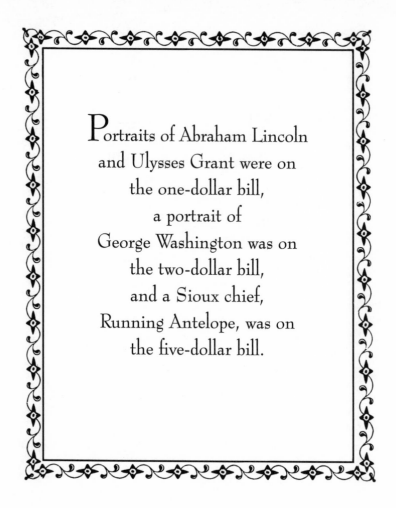

Portraits of Abraham Lincoln
and Ulysses Grant were on
the one-dollar bill,
a portrait of
George Washington was on
the two-dollar bill,
and a Sioux chief,
Running Antelope, was on
the five-dollar bill.

The Electropoise—a home medical device that strapped around the ankle and sent a mild electric current through the body—was sold as a cure-all for everything from the common cold to malaria. "Without a doubt," the ads asserted, "the Electropoise has the gift and power to cure multitudes who without it would surely die."

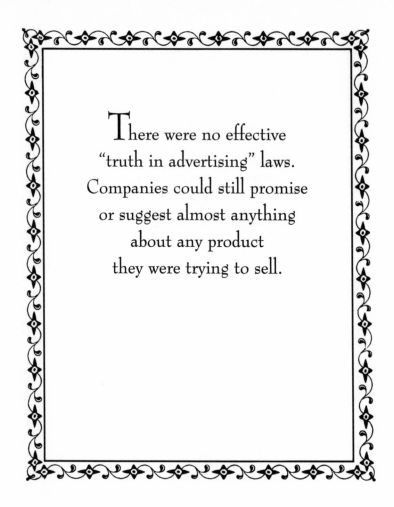

There were no effective
"truth in advertising" laws.
Companies could still promise
or suggest almost anything
about any product
they were trying to sell.

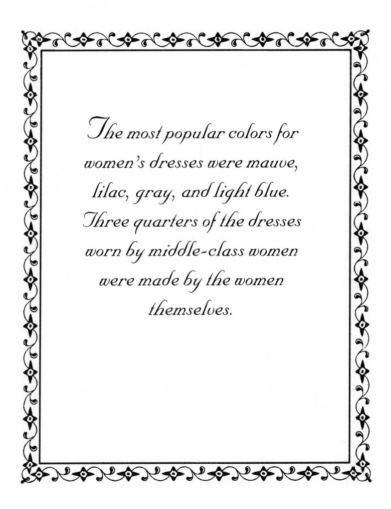

The most popular colors for women's dresses were mauve, lilac, gray, and light blue. Three quarters of the dresses worn by middle-class women were made by the women themselves.

Geranium and poppy petals were commonly used by women to stain their lips pretty colors. In big cities, wealthier women sometimes had their cheeks permanently tattooed in order to maintain the appearance of a constant rosy pink blush.

Eighteen percent of the homes in the United States had at least one full-time servant or domestic.

Renowned American architect Stanford White had just completed the lavish five-story Stuyvesant Fish mansion on East Seventy-eighth Street in Manhattan. The extravagant home—referred to locally as "the Palace of the Doges"—had thirty-five rooms, among them the largest ballroom (private or public) in New York City. Mrs. Fish described her new house as "an uncomfortable place for anyone without breeding."

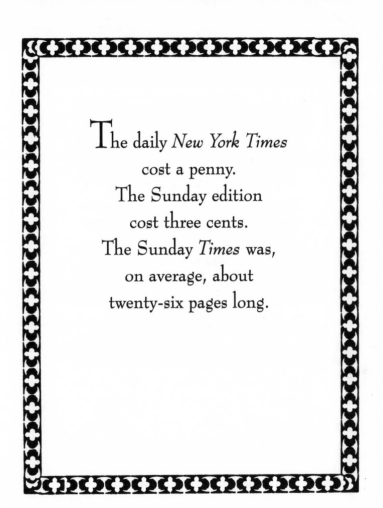

The daily *New York Times*
cost a penny.
The Sunday edition
cost three cents.
The Sunday *Times* was,
on average, about
twenty-six pages long.

In New York City, Mrs. Martha Grant of 80 Cherry Street accused a neighbor, Mr. Paul Martin, of having lured her pet dog, Spots, away from home with "choice meat morsels" and then detaining the animal against its will. A judge decided the case by ordering Spots released into the courtroom to see which of the two disputing parties he'd run to. "With a joyous yelp," a reporter wrote, "Spots immediately rushed over to his old owners, thus deciding beyond a doubt to whom he owed allegiance." COURT TOOK DOG'S TESTIMONY was the headline in the next day's *Times*.

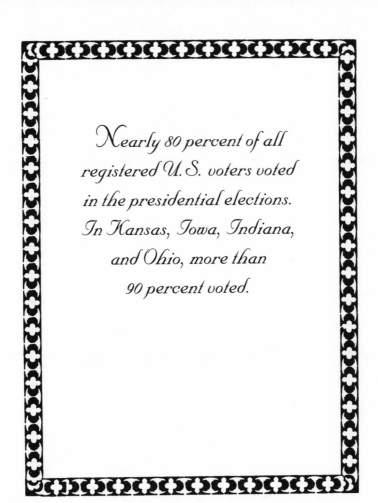

Nearly 80 percent of all registered U.S. voters voted in the presidential elections. In Kansas, Iowa, Indiana, and Ohio, more than 90 percent voted.

There were only 374,000 people in the United States over the age of eighty.

Major newspapers regularly
ran ads from spiritualists and
mediums who promised to
put people in touch with their
deceased loved ones.
The Ouija board—introduced
in the United States just
eight years earlier—
was wildly popular.

Americans smoked four billion cigarettes annually. However, pipes, cigars, and chewing tobacco were still more popular, as cigarettes were generally regarded as a bit effeminate by American men. The national Anti-Cigarette League moved to have cigarette smoking banned from all public places, and employees of the Union Pacific railroad were prohibited from smoking cigarettes after the railroad's president decided that cigarettes turned people into "fiends" and "lunatics."

There were about 230
reported murders
in the country annually.

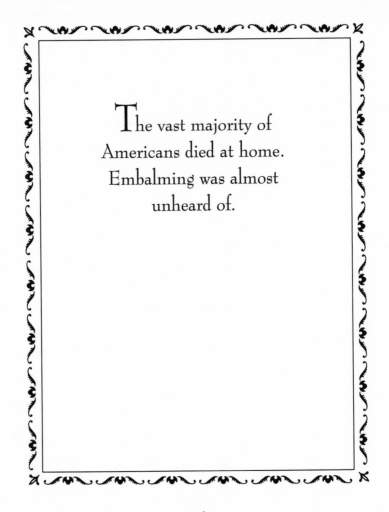

The vast majority of
Americans died at home.
Embalming was almost
unheard of.

Cemeteries weren't regarded as grim or unhappy places to be shunned by the living. Families often packed picnic lunches and went to cemeteries on weekends to enjoy themselves outdoors and socialize with other picnicking families.

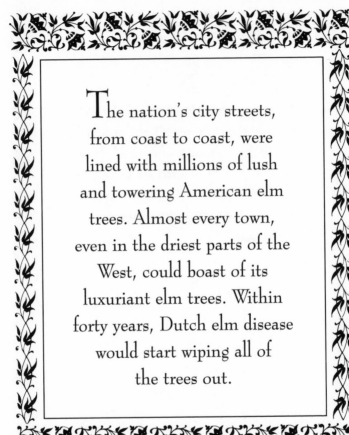

The nation's city streets, from coast to coast, were lined with millions of lush and towering American elm trees. Almost every town, even in the driest parts of the West, could boast of its luxuriant elm trees. Within forty years, Dutch elm disease would start wiping all of the trees out.

An increasingly misanthropic Mark Twain, now in his sixties and spending part of the summer in London, wrote pessimistically of the upcoming twentieth century: "The future is blacker than has been any future which any person now living has tried to peer into."

Science fiction writer H. G. Wells predicted in a magazine article that homes would soon come equipped with electric central heating, air conditioning, electric vacuum cleaners, self-making beds, and other astonishing labor-saving amenities. He would later write of the future of humanity, "I have come to believe in the greatness of human destiny. Worlds may freeze and suns may perish, but I believe there stirs something within us now that can never die."